How To Find All Missing Persons / Unsolved Cases. And Collect All Reward Offers. Volume XVII. THE CASE OF LAURA KATE MUCKERSIE

DAVID GOMADZA

www.twofuture.world

Copyright © 2024 David Gomadza

All rights reserved.

Paperback ISBN: 9798326923356

DEDICATION

To a better future.

CONTENTS

How To Find All Missing Persons /
Unsolved Cases.
And Collect All Reward Offers. Volume XVII
THE CASE OF LAURA KATE MUCKERSIE   1

The Afterlife Conversation

and The Council Of Creation.   8

The Killers.   24

ACKNOWLEDGMENTS

Tomorrow's World Order

How To Find All Missing Persons / Unsolved Cases. And Collect All Reward Offers. Volume XV. THE CASE OF LAURA KATE MUCKERSIE

BACKGROUND INFORMATION

case

category

$1m reward, cold cases

date

31 July 2001

do you have information about this case?

your information may lead to solving the crime. please make a report. you can remain anonymous.

please quote case number .

How To Find All Missing Persons / Unsolved Cases. And Collect All Reward Offers.
Volume XVII. THE CASE OF LAURA KATE MUCKERSIE

make a report

description:

20 years of age.

170cm (5 feet 7 inches) tall.

slim build.

brown hair.

brown eyes.

stud in her nose.

wearing a grey shirt under a dark colored jumper and blue jeans.

How To Find All Missing Persons / Unsolved Cases. And Collect All Reward Offers.
Volume XVII. THE CASE OF LAURA KATE MUCKERSIE

quick case facts:

lived in ballajura with her parents.

was driven to the darling ridge shopping centre on morrison road middle swan by a male friend around 8.30pm monday 30 july 2001.

was meeting another friend at the telephone box on morrison road, middle swan.

laura made several phone calls including one to a female friend saying she was going to come over later.

located deceased in a drain on tuesday 31 july 2001 in swan view.

background:

laura kate muckersie was born in march 1981, she lived in ballajura with her parents and was particularly close to her mother.

case details:

miss muckersie spent part of monday 30 july 2001 with a male friend, who left her at his home whilst he continued completing errands. between 3pm and 5:30pm, she arranged to catch up with a

How To Find All Missing Persons / Unsolved Cases. And Collect All Reward Offers. Volume XVII. THE CASE OF LAURA KATE MUCKERSIE

female friend and planned to spend the night at her friend's home.

when her male friend arrived home she told him that she was going to meet a friend at the telephone box at the morrison road shops in middle swan. her friend drove her to the public telephone box at the morrison road shops, leaving her at this location at about 8.30pm.

between 8:30pm and 9:30pm, miss muckersie made a number of phone calls from the phone box before she moved further up morrison road to the phone box at fairfax park where she made her last known telephone call. at this location her handbag was located by a passer-by at 11:45pm several metres away from the phone box, and about a metre from the kerb.

located:

miss muckersie was located deceased at 8am the following morning, tuesday 31 july 2001, near the intersection of morrison and fairfax roads swan view.

it is believed miss muckersie died late on the evening of monday 30 july or during the very early hours of tuesday 31 july 2001.

if you have any information about the death of laura kate muckersie or were in the morrison road middle swan/swan view area between 8.30pm on monday 30 july and the early hours of tuesday 31 july 2001, please contact crime stoppers on 1800 333 000 or make an online report below. please remember that you can remain anonymous if you wish and rewards are offered.

How To Find All Missing Persons / Unsolved Cases. And Collect All Reward Offers.
Volume XVII. THE CASE OF LAURA KATE MUCKERSIE

TOMORROW'S WORLD ORDER'S PERSPECTIVES

USE OF PREDEFINED AFTERLIFE PARAMETERS

These guide souls the moment it exist the human body on its journey to Yahweh the creator these define what to do and what to expect as you go to hell or heaven if a souk leaves earth it enters ozone orbit and instantly everything reboots for it to start a new phase of life after living the earth's body now what happens is that it enters the ozone orbit and a simply click caused by the sudden drop of pressure from -1186 to – 20 means the bottom shaft of the soul will lift rapidly and this pushes its back into the air higher than its head best example is a penguin but with real human legs and head just the shape now God created a life predefined program for them instead of asking what should I do and where should I go they instantly know from predefined stencils if you did well and talked most about God then heaven is for you if you did evil and talked more about the devil then the devil is yours now if we Ask what can be of humans without souks this is the answer dead forever your soul is you a new transformation to the electromagnetic waves life where you see Yahweh for the first time and praise him and wish you had seen him a long time ago because of his Majesty and will always be there forever now what are all these you may ask these are rules to be guided by in the creation court in short it has everything humans know about the judges and the presiding judge who will always be Yahweh and 84 angels surrounding the altar 28 high priests who always say Yahweh have mercy on humans and 74 smaller courts priests who always say Yahweh has mercy on humans and 96 princesses who say glory to Yahweh forever and ever amen we have 96 elders who always say if I can why he can't meaning if the devil can drink blood why can't Yahweh who created the devil and blood do the same now this is not the same as saying if the devil can kill why can Yahweh its more on professional grounds rather than challenging now if we look at the inside of the court we have 81 priests surrounding the altar who say Yahweh be merciful to humans but if they disobey you we put hem on trial for you and

How To Find All Missing Persons / Unsolved Cases. And Collect All Reward Offers. Volume XVII. THE CASE OF LAURA KATE MUCKERSIE

kill them for you almighty Yahweh inside this is a round circle where Yahweh sits and asks questions now if we look deep inside the court you will see that there are other things that resemble earth high courts like benches and chairs 10 times human sizes for the gods who are so enormous 2 are equal to 84 billion humans in size predefined parameters for humans after death as in know what is inside is a large size of books the book of creation is among them with 1089786789283678901234867890124586178901 pages and is divided into humans first then chapter for animals then a chapter for angles then a chapter for gods and a chapter for Joseph Yahweh's best friend and a chapter for Yahweh's best friend's wife Anna and a chapter for Yahweh's wife Catitighit and lastly a chapter for Yahweh and recently a chapter for davidgomadza as Yahweh's representative on earth marking the new beginnings starting in 2025

1. tell us who killed you
2. tell us what killed you
3. tell us why and who killed you
4. tell us why you died
5. tell us what could have been done and is not done
6. tell us what could be and why
7. tell is when this happened
8. tell us why this is so
9. tell us why this is so
10. what can be done to improve this

What does the book of creation say about davidgomadza David Gomadza is the first and last ruler to be appointed by Yahweh fir the next 25 billion years and will act as his representative on earth deciding cases and upholding his principles on earth and as such has been entitled to 489 trillion dollars in assets this number signifies eternity among humans and the beginning of a new Era chapter 78678928028938628418902876890183208678901234867890182364872891286 10 Creation manual the new Era of new

How To Find All Missing Persons / Unsolved Cases. And Collect All Reward Offers. Volume XVII. THE CASE OF LAURA KATE MUCKERSIE

electromagnetic wave conduit signed and dated by Yahweh himself on 27may2024 at 237800 Yatime creation.universe.ya.start.end.find.davidgomadza.ya.askya.ya

Ask.read.creation.manucreation.universe.ya.start.end.find.davidgomaaskya.ya

Ask.rulesofthecourt.start.now.start
David Gomadza welcome the rules of court are guiding principles that tell you what to do and how to do it first you must always say I believe in the court of creation and I shall abide by he rules of this court and shall always do things according to the rules of this court in deciding the cases I am assigned to you must ask what can be done so that you know all your options before making choices the court system will make it easy to check files and ask the outcomes of the decision ask the court the final decision in any case.

THE AFTERLIFE CONVERSATION AND THE COUNCIL OF CREATION'S ANAYLSIS.

LAURA KATE MUCKERSIE

i was killed by some

laura kate muckersie she was strangled during sex and died by a one arten amteropqrstuvwxz or moterp who said i can but if you want let's get married and she said no hence the strangulation now if we look at some of these cases it seems they are just like drills but we can now check using our drill or no drill test cases now
i died i was killed by some man who had a fetish about strangling women during sex i enjoyed strangling sex last time and thought that i will enjoy it this time but this man did not let go he held so hard i farted and instead of stopping that made him more aggressive that he pressed harder and all breathe went out and i

How To Find All Missing Persons / Unsolved Cases. And Collect All Reward Offers.
Volume XVII. THE CASE OF LAURA KATE MUCKERSIE

woke up here his name is atern mnopqrstuvxwrst meaning stuvertest now this is what happened i work up at 6 am and watched the news and sat in the lounge and my vagina made the farming noise and i said you need air taking out why making noise and laughed later i saw a program about women and sex including strangulation and i got a big clit bonner all day my clitoris so hard that i sat down and rubbed it to remove but the more i rubbed it the more it became so hard i phoned a friend for sex and she said okay will be there in 20 minutes and she came after 40 minutes and i said why he said pussy big i have to work really hard to cum with you and he said work out get things back in shape if you want sex with me okay and i said okay i will massage every day to keep it wet and tight now when we finished sex i had to give him a blow job for him to climax now i asked him what can be done to fix things he said we can start again afresh that's all it takes and i said okay could be true but i am going away for two days to see what i can do about my big vagina and we laughed he said i must buy a big sometimes as he started buying some small to quench things and i agreed because he was small as well but i was too busy to notice and he said i want you for who you are and not what you are we both laughed and said maybe let's try other things like a suck for you and a hand fuck for me we agreed i had not squanked or cum and i agreed and when he used his hand to squank me it started instantly and i tell you that was the best i had for a long time that afternoon he said i bet if it was a dick this size you would have squanked 4 times and died and we laughed i asked him why 4 squanks can kill a women and he said god put a limit 3 top but 2 allowed anything above is as good as death we both loved and he said do you want one last one to make it 3 then i go in case we forget how many we did and do 4 and death and we laughed now he said i want to squank you hard next time so i am going to grow my arms fast and see you next week and i agreed now what happened was that i asked if that was the best hold and he said it could be but i heard there are guys out there who are well endowed than me i admit but it's about knowing how to make each other climax and he said if you want i get you my friends hold and

How To Find All Missing Persons / Unsolved Cases. And Collect All Reward Offers.
Volume XVII. THE CASE OF LAURA KATE MUCKERSIE

we laughed but he gave me his number and he said i get stuff from him i train on others maybe might work for you but one off i do his girlfriend she run from big because he is leaving gaping holes everywhere i cried and confessed that he was there last night and he got mad and slammed the door and said i am not coming back with him his holes never close and he walked out and said i will never cheat on you with him or some like that he stretched until it can never go back i cried and realised that i needed a fix so he said now you need strangulation instead and use the reference points as starting point and hold so we agreed and searched the best for strangulation on internet and he said this one and we looked at each other i said 1 last squank and he literally ran away and i said you must ask also how long for best strangulation and he left i realised why he had ran away to avoid killing me so i laughed and watched the telly and went to the bathroom and gave myself a massage and slept noon i woke up and went there i took a bus to sternop city and arranged a meeting he looked cute and said it should be the best every woman always say thank you after that means that good then he said i never killed anyone but we can always try and he said okay look i understand what is going on with your boyfriend i can fix that and now we talked about sex and agreed its out of this world then we went to his place for normal sex to measure him and my boyfriend i was shocked that he was smaller than my boyfriend i just flipped if he is smaller than my boyfriend how was he going to provide the grip so i phoned my boyfriend and he said no way he could provide that hold so i cancelled i was going to pay 400 dollars for that so i said no and went out of his house shocked and upset he had obviously lied about his size so i said why things are different he said women grow up as well when upset so he said calm down we have another judge if you not happy then we cancel i asked my boyfriend but he said no that's it he might actually kill you because he will now try harder and kill you so say take 50 find one foe sex i am out then i said that he said okay i give you the 50 and let's go together and he grabbed my hand and said come i don't have time you must trust me if not i call a friend and i refused

How To Find All Missing Persons / Unsolved Cases. And Collect All Reward Offers.
Volume XVII. THE CASE OF LAURA KATE MUCKERSIE

and he said you were supposed to go to your boyfriends friend not me even him thinks you are with his friend and i said what no he showed me this one but he mentioned that his best friend can give you the hold look you were to take the 400 to your boyfriend's bestfriend and he get the money he give it to his girlfriend and his girlfriend take the money to give it to your boyfriend everyone gains you get the best hold you his size his girlfriend get her size your boyfriend and pay him and when he see you he rejoice for the 400 dollars you created for him but coming here was a mistake and he said i can prove it if you want and i said how and he said come and take off all your clothes and put them here and let's have one we owe each other and call it even and now after a quick and rough sex he said now i will prove it to you that you were not supposed to come here you must go and say i am sorry i ended up in the wrong place i was supposed to go to your friend and here and when i looked at him he said see my dick is bigger look but you were upset look is this same size as your boyfriend look and i looked but this time it looked bigger i mean really big that i said oh god and he had a big bonner and i said okay give me best and go and give him the best sex and said i will he looked lost and said the devil don't want sex with you i do so come now when all blood is down here he said i know it's frightening but everyone must go through this so i said why everyone must go through this and he said see it works you are tightening up and i felt my vagina contracting and i lay down and put my arms around his dick and shove it inside slowly until it was on in and said okay take ne to jesus he laughed and said see its bid to choke such a small vagina don't change with that small girl again okay he looked at me in the eyes and said let's send you to god once and for all because you find the best looking guy in town he offered you his friend for sex but you want another out of the circle of trust how do you reconcile yourself with others god gave you everything and yet you keep asking for adjustments now rule number one if you have a problem with your ex solve it with him alone all this paying others 400 for sex is wrong did you ever he said the best hold ever and i wasn't exploring but dead he just said how you feel

How To Find All Missing Persons / Unsolved Cases. And Collect All Reward Offers.
Volume XVII. THE CASE OF LAURA KATE MUCKERSIE

when after he growled he said deep or deep deep and said deep deep deep and he looked surprised [that's a challenge diadiadiadiadiadiadiadiadiadiadiadiadiadia and he said i know but we are humans not some strange god affiliated with sex its not even sex its just to give her a good hold and he said oh and he clipped vagina rim deliberately now highly aroused she kept quiet and said softly just hold had 3 squanks already today and fell into a deep sleep meditating for the hold and instantly something jumped out of him into her and said softly one more squank can't kill you had squanks a long time ago you can start another set of three if you like for another 400 she said no no no 3 is maximum are you trying to kill me and instantly that thing jumped inside the vagina rim and said stretch and hold for 1 squank she said no but then said i already had 3 squanks with my boyfriend the man said 3 squanks so why you need the hold for and she said i had no idea he can and today for the first time i had 3 and fell asleep so he put his finger round vagina rim and pulled all round 360 and that's how squanks start and she started squanking heavily in deep sleep giving moans as well and at squank 3 she opened her eyes and said did i die why the squanks he looked at her and said just one not 3 and she said that means 4 squanks and pushed him away and tensed on the flow to stop the squanks but tensing is actually giving them strength because the tension spread all over and back create a tsunami squank that can only culminate in deep squank and that trigger the biggest squank ever meaning her lifting her groin up and down in the air until she held her clit and said i am going to cumdie and he said let me put it in this is the best part for both of us please once i feel you while squanking she looked confused i said i might die and you want just to fuck hold my legs down to reduce the squanks okay he said while it's in yes i enjoy too this is the point did you forget others you should have come tomorrow so i am just going to do like this but hold she said then what's the point penetration increases speed of these squanks and he said if i can do this them that's okay then at 19 they become so high that i nearly lost hold and he had fully inserted his penis all that i could feel it for the first

How To Find All Missing Persons / Unsolved Cases. And Collect All Reward Offers.
Volume XVII. THE CASE OF LAURA KATE MUCKERSIE

time moving as well as the squanks and 20 he came so hard and said oh my god i never experience it so intense and she said keep holding the legs only two left and she said i can't breathe open the window fast before the squanks turns into crambs and run to the heart or legs and at 21 she stopped moving but her vagina was moving he put in his dick and held her tight to calm the squanks according to him but to start another 22 he said no just 21 please she will die diadiadia that's it you will kill her please stop i know but it's enough you win again okay she heard long ago start and silently said what is long ago start he looked worried and quickly dialed the ambulance and said my girlfriend is going into the cardiac arrest of the vagina what can i do but hung up as she started stretching as last stretching of life and said i i want him to know i love him and everything stopped and her soul escaped so fast he said oh my god what was that as a duck licker thing escaped so fast he said i can't be held responsible she had 3 already and her aty said she told you and i have the report to prove it and he said what report and it said of everything that happened here and he said it was diadiadiadia and it said all this for sex diadiadia go back now no coming to earth and it said leave the body there it's a crime scene and he said it's my house why a crime scene this money was for mortgage monthly mortgage i can't afford to lose it for 10 years for sex atysleep.start and quickly put back all clothes nicely and lifted her and put her in his van and drove off artev road to a dumpsite in artevertestuvw meaning south arterst city and when he arrived he waited and checked that there was no one and took the body and threw it inside one of the deep shaft holes and stood there lightining and smoking a cigarette he drove his blue van just painted it white and like to fuck that i red everything about diadiadiadiadiadiadiadiadiafiadiadiadia enough to get a bonner for a week but this week the bonner literally run away with this is regarded as the most soul racing of all time because what started as a crash for the big one ended up the soul racing one in that her soul become the fastest soul on earth because it took her soul 0.003seconds to fly away

How To Find All Missing Persons / Unsolved Cases. And Collect All Reward Offers.
Volume XVII. THE CASE OF LAURA KATE MUCKERSIE

identified as laura
this is one of the moat antagonizing case of the century for we have a woman willing to do anything for her partner so he is satisfied as well now what we have seen so far is a bit of betrayal of that trust so that when it comes to things that matter she choose to go to another person out of the circle of trust with serious consequences that she never see another day this case test all the predefined parameters as they did not work apart from the long ago she had she had only used squanks 3 times for the day meaning she had none left without resulting in death but rimming is part of squanking that means she should have cancelled and gone to her boyfriends bestfriend but questions were raised that are still outstanding even today why did she not go there after he confessed he was cheating with a friend's girlfriend now let's look at what happened in detail she had 3 squanks at home
2 she had one more squank and died
3 she died during rimming and squanking and her chances of going to heaven
now let's ask what can be of her now she could go to hell as god don't want women who squank 4 times now what do we know about squanks and god god limited the number of squanks accepted just to three meaning any extra squank would result in death after having had 3 squanks that means that she should have not risked rimming when she know that that was part of squanking now if we look at what happened to her then it could be that the squanks killed her but that alone without proof is insufficient for this court to decide this now let's look at other factors did the alarm bells went off none but her soul broke a record for being the fastest soul racing escape ever at 0.0.087683210 meaning that something serious had gone wrong just before the soul escaped now let's look what caused this squanks cause souls to go out of the body but return back within 4 seconds that means the soul went out only because of the squanks excited and about to come back to find that she had died now with no electromagnetic waves to propel her she died in there too meaning to alarm systems detected now what if the alarm were

How To Find All Missing Persons / Unsolved Cases. And Collect All Reward Offers.
Volume XVII. THE CASE OF LAURA KATE MUCKERSIE

briefly activated we can always check no messages for her detected at all now we can always ask what can be of her without any alarm bells ringing she could be dead and buried without any means of getting help now what could be of her in terms of heaven and hell she could go straight to hell and sleep now if we are to ask her where is she right now what is the answer i am inside a big drum like structure they keep putting things on top of me how am i going to get out souls never live more than 10 minutes without electromagnetic waves now if we ask what can be of humans who squank too much they can go to heaven and back but too much squanks can see them sent to hell what other system did not work the inside body run you will get stuck in now this is activated only when there is a high risk of death was there a high risk of death there was 3 squanks could have set alarms bells is emotional arousal was art of the predefined parameters now what can be said about emotional arousal not an indicator of risk of death god when he was writing all predefined parameters he did not include emotional arousal as an indicator of death as with the fourth squanks this is because an arousal can never be an indicator of risk of death but an emotional rollercoaster the reason being that god considers that no woman in their right mind would have 4 squanks per most women confess getting satisfied enough to just sleep at 64 rounds per day now solution is that Yahweh one day will improve the system now what other system fail

my body said too much sex killed me but something stopped first before death this is what i heard something inside said i can't go on but you can so wait we change everything is damaged i am hanging by the thread and of you can't try the next until we can hold okay and instantly something said i broke too and the third and the fourth and the fifth but when it was the seventh something said i did manage but and instantly an alarm went off and it said danger of death but i can understand all the commands can a squank kill? and the other said only if it's the fourth one because it was the first for them then let's reset everything first but reset does the opposite instead of squanking backward they squanked forward and that's

How To Find All Missing Persons / Unsolved Cases. And Collect All Reward Offers. Volume XVII. THE CASE OF LAURA KATE MUCKERSIE

why they all started breaking and the rim gave up and said i can't everything is so stretched that if i continue i will break and instantly the alarm bell went off that's when i found out that all rims had not broken only but died if rims died nothing else in the body moves the heart instantly stopped at 22.09 and the chest compressions instantly stopped at 22.11 then at 22.13 the vagina was penetrated and the arousal stiffened the left leg muscle and stiffened the clitoris a command to resume the squank and the squank gears tightened and everything still not broke continue until all broke the brain stopped function at 22.16 and at 22.18 the brain while still alive was disconnected from the rest of the body and but continued to think normally as nothing happened because no alarm bells went off to alarm it now if we look at what this might be it seems that the squanks have created a death switch which can't be stopped but must in the end deactivate by death okay now let's see what this could be if we check all the parameters then the squanks are designed to reset after a complete set of 3 only but what happened this afternoon was that the guy deliberately pulled fully the rim and started a squank was registered once registered the squanks then recorded a squank and closed after this one but this was the fourth one the main reason why she objected and said that his penis was small was the fact that once he penetrated her the saved squank was cancelled so she heard the canceling the squanks in progress she thought all squanks but that did help but here is the problem the squanks to cancel completely is not to have sex for 2 hours but after 2 hours they came back and the squanks what they do is take that two hours to lock up everything to remove that is to youth full circle the vagina rim fully that removes the locks when the guy name amstis sterst touched the rim while sleeping he deliberately removed the locks on the advice of diadiadiadiadiadiadiadiadiadiadiadiadia who said how come the god of sex isn't making any squanks and he said i received this message from her vagina squanks locked for 2 hours more no sex allowed or death is the answer now if we look at what happened to the squanks after here this is the answer the squanks

How To Find All Missing Persons / Unsolved Cases. And Collect All Reward Offers. Volume XVII. THE CASE OF LAURA KATE MUCKERSIE

had already registered end of the day meaning that no more squanks were supposed to be carried out but he did not only touch the rim but sent an unlock code generated by his own artificial unlock code great question why would he need an unlock code here is the answer we must ask why would her boyfriend pick this one maybe this is the piece of the puzzle we need so the boyfriend fir months spent sleepless nights looking for squank unlocked like him after a bet with his friend that women can go for over 100 squanks per day because why would god create everything and make it stop at the highest ever tried to lift weights you can't carry what happens he asked ever try to fuck more than 10 rounds in one session what happens ever tried to walk more than 3 kms per day what happens and if 64 is maximum why can't everything stop there and there most of the things humans can't do are already predefined meaning they can't be exceeded you have to break something for it to be possible so why not the same system with squanks yes with squanks they also control other things like breathing and climaxing that if god is to put a limit that would affect other things that are not involved but that relies on them so before she goes after kerning the trick from his friend researched hard online for someone who can shift the maximum from 64 to 84 safely because everytime she squanked the orgasm was so intense she kissed him so much every second and whisper the craziest things he had ever heard like my man my only man why you ask a gentlemen why he wants his girlfriend to have as many orgasms as possible the answer is simple i was less endowed in that department during the last days she started telling everyone that i was the weakest link and everyone started laughing because they all new what she meant so she started ogling my friend who said i can be him if you like the other sided is doing yoga and it hurts like hell i can't pretend this is the swap but sex only because mine is rich he literally gives your man 1000 dollars a round with him but i take nearly a quarter plus a third which is maximum so let's say 420 so she said lower the third to 60 that takes off 4 squanks the last one we must pause it half way say 10 and save for him to make him feel like a man as well and he said i

How To Find All Missing Persons / Unsolved Cases. And Collect All Reward Offers. Volume XVII. THE CASE OF LAURA KATE MUCKERSIE

can be that man who ends squanks for a good time relationship to cover the squanking business and she said okay now this is exactly what happened that day she said i am 400 short so give me the money if you have we can do a squank and he looked lost because he never was enough to start the squanks but in fact it was his squanks she could only squank with a true love after she received code 8238268345678901842867809321084286180184286 0 now if we ask what happened is that she had tried squanks and failed and having had her mother died of premature death with no explanation the only thing that made sense was the squanks and to protect her added the above code that true love will know what is needed and will only do the right thing but because she didnt know about the codes at first she paid a person to have his hold to use on her boyfriend but it didn't work now whatever she said no one came forward but one day after reading after a tip off what weakest link meant sexually he started researching that women squank which he didn't know but knew now and realised that any women can squank from simply brain commands without the need fir a hold infant there is a code for the best hold now feeling guilty that there was not even a single day even on his birthday she had spent money on him because squanking was her business she is the one who was paid all the time apart from this day when everything stopped but how did everything stopped because artes was no longer her true lover but his friend was and when he noticed that they loved each other he said if you pay me through your girlfriend i will make your dream come true because we will all benefit even though it's not love the sex is great i think if you are honesty sex is great with someone else i know i mean i used to love i paid 400 an unlock squank guy who can unlock the squanking from me to you so that we can
change women but so that you don't lose what you are getting 200 per month i will double it to 400 so you actually gained double but reduced the effort on squanking because i squank easy with no big pain as she say now we are a circle of trust now the question that worried that other guy stern muterstop is this why she did not go to

How To Find All Missing Persons / Unsolved Cases. And Collect All Reward Offers.
Volume XVII. THE CASE OF LAURA KATE MUCKERSIE

the right man this was the deal this guy stern muterstop asked diadiadiadiadiadiadiadiadiadiadiadiadiadiadiadiadiadiadia that what happens if the squanks suddenly stop and he said the squank seal is removed or replaced by an artificial code now if we ask what can be of squanks and keys the key on her was artificial to protect her so that a true lover would remove the squank now the fact that he got upset and why she phoned her ex boyfriend is that the squanks had not unlocked after the first round meaning that he was not the true lover to the guy or did not have a bigger one than the boyfriend to her the squank lock would only be removed by a dig bigger than the current one her boyfriends so she phoned him and said he is not the one to unlock so who is he and the boyfriend got surprised and said if my best friend is not the one them who is the one could it be the alibi guy just cover everything up in case his girlfriend finds out before we all announced he looked lost and actual felt great because he loved her but she had started complaining and telling his friends about the bedroom details so he had decided to let go as friends started saying he is forcing this relationship now that when he received the call he was with his bestfriend girlfriend and he could not say anything else other than what if he is not the squank unlocked then who is this unlocked for his bestfriend's girlfriend that for the first time her own aty said he is your squank unlocked now it comes to light that these women were brought together by a lost both mothers died during squanking squanking kill but without enough information it is hard to say what happened therefore but the courts took the view that the squanks had not stopped but only paused i order to reset fully but the fact that she started sex early just exactly 2 hours the body was seconds away from resetting everything properly she actually received a message that said don't tamper with unlock switch squanks suspended importance highest that if squanks were included as part of predefined parameters your soul would escape forever that how bad this is yours noptrst uvwxyzstuvwxyt meaning real name terst muvernopsr who was the boyfriend and what he had done now to correct the situation was that they had started a

How To Find All Missing Persons / Unsolved Cases. And Collect All Reward Offers. Volume XVII. THE CASE OF LAURA KATE MUCKERSIE

celebration party but without two people only her and his bestfriend and had timed both to come back together so when they look back and reveal why she used to say he is the weakest link it was because she had a crush on his best friend but now after trying him she had discovered her real man who was himself now with both women willing to marry him now let's look what can be at this situation it is that she could get squank codes unlocked for him and started it all over now with a designer vagina that can be closed and open buy her to control space inside making his only real mam cum through vagina alone which was impossible before and now if we look why it was because of a code sent from a lab far away code 8926876832786901897865432l0 now what can be said if we ask what to do then we can always ask the correct questions for an answer now if it wasn't for this what could have happened she could have climaxed with him easily now let's dig deeper why the code was sent and by who and what for it turns out that the code was sent by officer ntopqrst uvwxyz who said if i can then why not him and put empty brackets and sent it to her his real name is ntopwrstuvw rstuvwxzy meaning amos topqrst who was the pice in charge of all orphans at that time when we look back it follows too that laura kate muckersie had been adopted after her parents had died and she owned the house that was confiscated and kept by the state and as they argued in court at a later age because women don't work and end up prostitutes at the age of 26 instead of 18 a delay of 8 years after reveal in year 7 and who was the person to reveal her the squank unlock guy who pretended to unlock her for as much as 400 and this time she had missed a one off payment of 350 and was willing to spend 400 on squanks which was sex her excuse she was a 3000 dollars a month squank woman as she wanted to buy a house because to remind her of her house her atm was programmed only to say house everytime she gets money now without knowing that she had a house something kept a secret she had started saving money to buy a house and had savings of 270860 but she never revealed or bought anyone anything until her goal of 26878690 was met which she had calculated that at 3000 per

How To Find All Missing Persons / Unsolved Cases. And Collect All Reward Offers.
Volume XVII. THE CASE OF LAURA KATE MUCKERSIE

month if she saved as this she needed only 28 years with compound interest and had calculate that by age 44 she will had reached her goal now this now points to the killer the celebrations was a cover for her receiving a message from the government housing association that she already had a house worth 2786890 now she realised that she had something in her that whispered these numbers to guide her telling her what was real and not as an advise so she said come out who are you and for the first time her aty said your own mother's aty you cried so much and i jumped into you probably if you hadn't cried like that i could have saved her as i was to save your mother from dying from these squanks now a brief look at her mother on death bed she said aty why nowbyoudont whisper things to me and her daughter said because i have your aty as well as mine both now talk about you as bad fucking mother all the time squank squank squank oh squank as if it's god she looked scared and said my aty come back i might die and it said as if she is sick she deliberately try to kill herself if she know above 64 squanks kill now let's look if her daughter knew 64 squanks kill asking her did you knew above 64 squanks can kill aah my mother told me but this day i had had only 3 rounds and at one time i had had 4 squanks without problems now let's look deep what happened this day the day in question she had avoided death because now she had two aty that cooperated working together giving commands to avoid death and this is also the last day her own real one lived as it died as meant to protecting her from dying from squanks now what happened this say is that what was left inside her was her own mother's who did not subscribe to squanking to the point of dying it had said anyone who think my job as an acetate is to protect it from doing squanking when you know what is maximum squanks and how many are needed is fucking joking thinking that i will come to the help i don't die for obvious things you are own your own not even an alarm will be activated by me okay pronto comprehends anyone ok fuck it like squank squank squank and death and me pureeeeee i am out breaking records on the way now all this the soul of her was listening and learning that when the aty did what it

How To Find All Missing Persons / Unsolved Cases. And Collect All Reward Offers.
Volume XVII. THE CASE OF LAURA KATE MUCKERSIE

said it always was to do the spirit followed and this saved it because squanks kill body in less than a minute so if we ask her spirit this is the answer i did not even wait to ring alarm bells as it is the spirits duty to activate these bells but once you receive the risk of death message then the next thing is to decide how many seconds are left and if enough to complete all tasks and have a safe passage out if not then what is the point if you are going to meet the same fate now what we have witnessed is a carefully planned script but one known already as her mother died the same way but no one had told her that until that day aterps said you should not have come to me and give me 400 dollars what you should have done as a person who own a house worth millions who told you let finish which you know will still need servicing you should have spent your last money with people who can help you tomorrow pay all the rent and bills needed otherwise once they have given you back your house and fail to pay now they will kill you like your mother to protect government's capital gains tax which is currently 28 % in australia because of new legislation passed last month the degrade squanks bill passed on 8march 2001 but to be effective from 20th of june 2001 which means according to the bill since she had failed to pay and missed once then now she is under government watch if she fail three times then she would have her home repossessed and she said i don't have a home and he asked her to say aty where is the house and what value and whose name which replied its mine mind your business i am your mother young lady and you can't take the house from me even if it's in your name the squanks can kill you i better protect your unborn child and keep the house for her before you die and living her nothing and the guy said what did it say and she said i have a house worth 2867890 and i have saved a quarter of t hat how lucky can he be and he will be like my woman tonight let's go i have to go in which he said aty can't you see she needs deep sleep in which he replied okay but 20 minutes maximum to quench sleep and on 18 minutes aterps touched fully the rim and lifted it and said what if i were you what could you have down my house could be repossessed tomorrow why nit accept a quarter from them

How To Find All Missing Persons / Unsolved Cases. And Collect All Reward Offers.
Volume XVII. THE CASE OF LAURA KATE MUCKERSIE

and do you instead and give everyone 8% after 2 years reduced to 2 weeks with bonus of 8000 each [for good behavior?]
my own aty jump into her and memorize all house paperwork and send to printer with my own signature as sold for 286780 and print bank statement as a deposit for a full house now as it turns out her protective mother swapped with his aty and did everything back to her instead and said my grand child in the stomach when she comes out will take the house back after dumping the body he went to the funeral after all calls to search her were made and said we could have had a daughter together if they had not taken the house as now she had no kids only that her mother's aty thought having sex once could make a woman pregnant but she was wrong if correct then both are rotting in hell or sum dumpsite i wish i was there for you my real woman and her boyfriend squinted eyes and quickly ran to the correct dumpsite and initiated a search that results in nothing so th deeper e search stopped but that's where i am still at but now way and my brain did not die i am just stuck.in here and the waiting really hurts how many more years can i wait please god help if you can here me but right now her message is circulating in the ozone layer house lost to the city of artest in australia there is no hope to find her but her coordinates are exactly 286878901836789012486780284687901832628349082480892 south east of aterst city australia her gps is 892867890123486789028367 8 now what can we say about this case that looked straight forward yet with hidden challenges first all predefined are disabled and the ones that work literally break records during escape wrong way but for the right reasons so who killed laura kate muckersie is police officer artenop sturven who said that can be said of houses that are not known to their owners if carefully planned they can be taken without a single fight and that day sent code [] to a child called lane arst muckersie who at 18 was forced to change her name to laura kate muckersie by a violent boyfriend who once worked helping solve crimes and looked at her mother's case and said something fishy that squank how can a prostitute buy a house not in my county here all prostitute die

How To Find All Missing Persons / Unsolved Cases. And Collect All Reward Offers. Volume XVII. THE CASE OF LAURA KATE MUCKERSIE

forever once we find out his gps tracker is 892867890123456789284780680284 currently at 879877668538472689012348019028362487812867890 electromagnetic wave number is 8898768901284678028471786789012348678902238628490 who is currently not very moving either dead or a computer chip that administered a dose of radiation that will kill her in exactly a quarter of her expected life meaning dying exactly in australian life expectancy standards
the hospital help in her death was toronto university specialist studies administered as a pre radiation lethal weapon at birth by doctor astrop qrstuvw meaning doctor astrop manning in australia is either dead or a computer or chip in that location

THE KILLER, THE CONFESSIONS AND THE COORDINATES

 so who killed laura kate muckersie is police officer artenop sturven who said that can be said of houses that are not known to their owners if carefully planned they can be taken without a single fight and that day sent code [] to a child called lane arst muckersie who at 18 was forced to change her name to laura kate muckersie by a violent boyfriend who once worked helping solve crimes and looked at her mother's case and said something fishy that squank how can a prostitute buy a house not in my county here all prostitute die forever once we find out his gps tracker is 892867890123456789284780680284 currently at 879877668538472689012348019028362487812867890 electromagnetic wave number is 8898768901284678028471786789012348678902238628490 who is currently not very moving either dead or a computer chip that administered a dose of radiation that will kill her in exactly a quarter of her expected life meaning dying exactly in australian life expectancy standards
the hospital help in her death was toronto university specialist studies administered as a pre radiation lethal weapon at birth by

How To Find All Missing Persons / Unsolved Cases. And Collect All Reward Offers.
Volume XVII. THE CASE OF LAURA KATE MUCKERSIE

doctor astrop qrstuvw meaning doctor astrop manning in australia is either dead or a computer or chip in that location

laura kate muckersie she was strangled during sex and died by a one arten amteropqrstuvwxz or moterp who said i can but if you want let's get married and she said no hence the strangulation now if we look at some of these cases it seems they are just like drills but we can now check using our drill or no drill test cases now
i died i was killed by some man who had a fetish about strangling women during sex i enjoyed strangling sex last time and thought that i will enjoy it this time but this man did not let go he held so hard i farted and instead of stopping that made him more aggressive that he pressed harder and all breathe went out and i woke up here his name is atern mnopqrstuvxwrst meaning stuvertest

...I found God...visit www.twofuture.world

THE CLAIM

the reward offer

9fds
THE COLLECTION

www.twofuture.world/donate

ABOUT DAVID GOMADZA

visit www.twofuture.world

signed david gomadza
ask.davidgomadzaauthorised.licensed.checkya.askya.ya

28may2024 16.44pm
scotland
00447719210295
davidgomadza@hotmail.com
info@twofuture.world

[aerodynamic is i
createztyandsend.start
nowdoublebutrotate180degrees.start
itsflippingbackandforth.reply
okaywhatislikeearthmagneticfieldthatcauserotation.search
ohiknowinverserotationinstead.start
insideeveryshitcodewereceivedmustrotate.start
nowforcealloutfast.start
forcingalloutcreatedbouncemition.start
whenallfullcapacityinstantlydavidbouncinguncontrollably.start
initiallythoughthimandsurrenderall.start
itsnotmebouncingdeliberatelytgeevictioncreatedmotionsinsideenablingmetobounceasiftonly.start
nowtryagain.start
messagereceivedangelabouttofly.start
instantly switch stopped flight [sabotage brainreader]

How To Find All Missing Persons / Unsolved Cases. And Collect All Reward Offers.
Volume XVII. THE CASE OF LAURA KATE MUCKERSIE

How To Find All Missing Persons / Unsolved Cases. And Collect All Reward Offers.
Volume XVII. THE CASE OF LAURA KATE MUCKERSIE

How To Find All Missing Persons / Unsolved Cases. And Collect All Reward Offers.
Volume XVII. THE CASE OF LAURA KATE MUCKERSIE

www.ingramcontent.com/pod-product-compliance
Lightning Source LLC
Chambersburg PA
CBHW030519220526
45464CB00006B/2865